What Must Go On

By

Chuck Harp

Published by Unsolicited Press

www.unsolicitedpress.com

info@unsolicitedpress.com

Unsolicited Press Books are distributed by Ingram.

Printed in the United States of America.

Attention schools and businesses: for discounted copies on large orders, please contact the publisher directly.

Editor: S.R. Stewart ; Sarah Keen

Cover Image: Aaron Vasco

Cover Design: UP Team

ISBN: 978-1-947021-28-0

Thanks To

Aaron Vasco for the cover art

Every friend who ever showed me a song

And

Phife Dawg R.I.P.

Poems

Green Room

Ripping his cigarette to the nub

the Front Man gazes at

scribbles by the natives,

the throat torn kings

that came before him.

Flicking the butt,

he stands at attention.

His smoke-stenched fingers squeeze

the microphone.

The empty room is puddled in whiskey stains

while past chaos hovers about

like the chalk lines

of street crime scenes

Crescendo.

A guitar riff tears through

the silence and snatches him from the space.

The glass sweats on the table,

and soaks the wood as

swiftly as the whiskey

disappears down his throat.

Head bowed he bolts for the door

both engulfed by cheers

and pelted with praise by his fans.

Late for the Dismantle

Blurring their faces like photography flash he barreled down

between gawkers and drunks. A guitar in the right hand,

a beer in the left.

The strap slid over his head

as he slammed the brew in hopes it would cool

his sweaty brow.

Faces gazed at him in awe,

awaiting the sound of thunder

to smother the silent sea.

His darting eyes scanned

shadow shaped silhouettes

before buckling his knees,

taking root in the wooden stage.

One strum

told who he was.

Two strums

gave warning to the lot.

Three strums

With no objections

a smiled flared from his lips

a fire blazed behind

his charcoal eyes.

Around the Fire

It was the call of the wild with the feedback screeching like a

banshee, clutching the crowd by the throat with her chilled

haunting hands.

He announced his arrival as if he was waving a banner.

He called forth his troops,

their name hissed across the hollow land, and readied them

for conquering.

Tonight was the night for mayhem.

Tonight was the night for pride.

His vocals lashed out around the room, sending shots to the

world that came back again.

The chorus chanted his commandments

and nailed them to their hearts.

Like a noose

they hung to every word

and mouthed every lyric:

Illustrated dreams,

Escape the siren screams!

Illustrated dreams,

Escape the siren screams!

The group was ordered to take hold of this world and claim it as their own. And above all, stick the flag firmly in what mattered most.

Edges Without Frames

Like hornets surround the nest
children of chaos ignite.
They've eaten their aggression
and cut away the lesions
time unfairly provides.
The hour is rich with fear,
brotherhood and debauchery
bursts through iron-clad gates.

A swarming sea of legs,
the pounding waves of fists.
Shouts grow louder
as the choppy waters collapse
upon the still shores.

Night shifters on the prowl
howl to the call
of their mad conductor.
Bystanders ignore the beware

for they feed on the energy

the meat of

calloused fists

and battered souls.

Moving Pictures

Almost stabbing the ceiling

his bass beat the crowd back. Fingers plucked and pounded,

like a desperate man clinging onto what ifs and maybes

he braced the neck.

As if it were his dance partner

He twirled the bass about

mimicking the swinging skirts before him.

Bringing the beat back he pieced together

old dusty photos

and the sounds of scratched vinyl.

And as swiflty as it started,

his dance runs out of steps.

The zoot suits died away

with the shimmering jazz-hall chandeliers.

He finds himself back in the era he was born into

instead of held in the one he belongs.

Chattering Toes

Sinking low,

low into the depths

of his starving pockets, cracked and bruised fingers filled

the empty space within.

He would sell his soul,

but even that

is out of stock.

Those sunken brown eyes see

no change,

just a litter of lint

and the same old sidewalks.

But covering his feet,

clicking along the pavement,

are his terribly scuffed tap shoes.

Heels to toes, drowning

out his roaring stomach.

They lead blistered feet to the park where the eyes wallow,

watching the dancing man

hope on the kindness of others.

An Old Black Hat

Just a hat by his feet.

The pan that he handled,

and the keeper of his coins.

The cover to a bald spot,

and the mask for his pride.

The voice in the alley-winds,

and prop in his curb-side play.

The shade from blistering rays,

and the glimmer in his eye.

Now just a hat by his feet.

Hung From the World

Pulling back the curtain,

the wooden figures danced

for the wide-eyed youth.

He practiced his voices,

swing dance and merengue.

The small stage loomed with the magic of pig-tailed guests.

No need for the silver screen.

Boy and girls were bystanders

Of an epic tale.

Immersing themselves

in pretend as if they were really there.

The heart strings,

to this visual love letter.

Thinner than the spine

but a backbone for the story.

Old tales from old countries

and now diluted cultures.

Friends in the Dark

Laughter is the best medicine.

It was more than a phrase

to her growing up alone

in that mysterious foreign orphanage

She always felt forever isolated among the many rooms

and frazzled faces about.

Sometimes she felt split,

like a war-beaten child.

A spirit broken,

a family torn apart

by the hands of stray bullets

and political strife.

She giggled at the diary pages that

became her map of the world. Breaking apart society's

structured formalities,

they kept her stuck

in the shell of her shadow.

But now the

muted murmurs

bring about brightness

to her dim, candle-lit room.

And the crowd,

howling with laughter

turned the key opening

her new home.

The Poor Sweet

She crawls along the bathroom floor licking
at her newest wounds.
Mona never knew him
but went along anyway.
The music beat to their hearts
and he was standing close
enough to touch.

It was the calm before the storm
and the sea was packed with fish.
Tension filled the air
with murmurs of teenage angst
pushing past the sweaty crowd
smells of teen spirit and old spice.

When the single dropped
they surrendered to a thirsty flame.
Let the taste of pain ooze
from their pores and rinse

them out onto the floor.

It was over before it started.

David, Jack, Henry or Stan.

It wasn't important anyway.

It was feelings amongst strangers,

like fingers between one another.

When the action fell

only that white sink remained.

That dull white porcelain

now covered in dirt and grime.

Halftime Show

Kenny lifts the beaten sticks

from his back pocket.

His fingers barely hanging on to splinters.

The old sun begins to rest

as beads run down his dark, thick neck.

A deep breath,

preps for the barrage of blows

to strike the egg-white bucket.

They mirror those self-inflicted combos caused by bad

memories that ruptured his hot head.

The vibrations violently slithered

down his bare arms,

as if ready to rape his wrists

and crack his fingernails.

Angie's Plan

Just a few more weeks, Angie lied to herself.

Just a few more weeks,

and I'm back even.

No more dark backroom lounges with wealthy old men

and their rusty hooks.

Smoke-spoiled hair

and a glittered chest,

washed away by the stale sweat-polluted smell of success.

A breath exited her lungs

as the name Cherry

excites the crowd

over flashing lights

and a booming bass.

The spotlight is like steaming sunrays

to a pale vampire bat.

She moved to the stage,

showcasing the shame

of glitter-lathered porcelain skin.

Baring all but the dread.

she quickly swallowed.

Just a few more weeks.

A Glass Jar and Wooden Box

A hint of blue leaked out onto the empty tables of

Jack's Bar Rag.

It was an older bar

resembling a bombed-out cathedral

more so than a drinking establishment.

Gracefully,

almost daintily,

Kate strummed the strings of her guitar, allowing the last

moments of her exposed soul to hover about the room.

It was lyrical graffiti,

ripping though sound waves

and plastering itself

against cheap painted purple walls.

Passion rose into the dank air

that sat in the room like smoke. Past pain,

lingering between the lines

of heavenly imagery

and pulsating thick shadows.

Her strong voice rattled the roof

making the glasses kiss their neighbors.

But when the last string was plucked

the drunkards in the back

sat dog-eyed with expressions chiseled from stone.

 Only a few slow claps echoed

from the torn leather booths.

She boxed up her dreams,

her tortured joy…

and grabbed the tip jar

before heading back home.

Just a Moment to Go

When the smoke clears and the lights dim low,

I'll paint my constitution in the lining of their ears.

I'll hand them my voice,

my words and expressions,

and let them twist the words to their will.

I'll give them the world,

my universe,

and leave them salivating.

A stillness will linger

above hundreds of shouting faces as they mimic my

       incantation.

I'll give them my hand,

my blessing and courage,

and beg them to stand with me.

The Mic

Silver

and stained with saliva,

it waits to grab whispers like pigeons on rooftops.

It is the translator of thought,

the guide of the spirit

toward the faithful listener that waits with an unquenchable

heart.

An Assassin At Work

Standing at five-foot nothing,
he's a mountain of an ant hill

He looms under soft lights
while the scream of applause
raise the dead-eyes below.

With plenty of guff given,
each line is a sword piercing the pride
in his opponent's heart. Words barrage the brain,
bruising fat egos
with constructed stories of guarded false pride.

In no time at all
he brings the man down to him, dismantling his strong will
snikt-snap, snikt-snap
slicing through the dense
smog of harsh truths.
The survivor lets his guard down,

now standing victorious above all

in this lyrical battleground.

A Night Before

Because he was told
wine had less calories,
the half-drank bottle dangled
from his bitten fingertips.
Loose lips opened wide
devouring the stream of cheap grapes
to drown a nervous stomach.

It beat away the thought of low lights, of red silk curtains
containing mystery.

The blare of [instruments] below,
manipulating man's emotions.
The caress of thin bows
skimming over strings.
Beautiful gleaming brass calling out.
Black and white keys dancing along
with the player's feet.
Love would bring him to the stage,

bring him home late nights with a sore voice from chorus

songs and swollen red feet from every demanding number.

Still, upon that living platform,

it would strike his gut

like a blow from a boxer.

It was medicine given from

what's hidden by dark curtains, relief that came with whistles

and claps, smiles and roses.

Break A Leg

Just drain the soul upon the stage.

Give the crowd their entertainment,

their hope and dismay.

Give the critics their career,

of power and pain.

Give the world their distractions,

that they so rightly need.

Just leave the soul upon the stage.

Passion Does Play

Sitting in the charred remains

of a now glassless church,

she stood above the makeshift stage trying to hold back fear

that crawled around inside of her.

Dressed in a black so dark

it rivaled the sitting shadows,

she welcomed the curious few

who made it past the chain-linked fence.

This is the moment

that has been slumbering in the gears of her heart.

A young girl's diary in motion poured from her mouth only

to be slurped up like soup.

Standing Ovation

Now the music fades.

Applause outgrow

the darkness like the rising tide.

Heat from the high lights fade

as The Group moves toward the

solitude of the cool darkness backstage.

It's

hard

to catch

one's breath

as the nerves still twitch

with adrenaline. Sitting by the curtain side voices can be

heard calling out for their heroes.

.

But before the last hand claps their presence fills

one more shining moment,

waving to the faceless few

who have left their seats empty.

Shows Over

He hears the floorboards of the stage creak below him

like a settling home

while his broom glides across

the flower covered wood paneling.

Remnants of thankful roses

still smashed the golden stage,

while the cheers from the crowd

sit on night air.

Lights from above shower down almost lifting him from

the ground.

Taking his old wooden broom

he twirls around with her,

whistling a tune as his hips sway.

About the Author:

Chuck is a writer with a barfly's sense of story who currently resides in Los Angeles. His work can be found at *101 Words, Queen Mob's Tea House, Public Pool,* and his book *Blooming Insanity* has been published with Dostoyevsky Wannabe.